The Void To Fill

S. N. Johnson

BookLeaf Publishing

Presentation by *BookLeaf Publishing*

Web: www.bookleafpub.com

E-mail: info@bookleafpub.com

ISBN: 978-93-95784-10-8

First edition 2022

DEDICATION

Em, Meech, Poobs, and Booke (The Big 4)
Momma Loves You

ACKNOWLEDGEMENT

I want to give appreciation and Thanks to my Sister Circle who have always been an ear, a shoulder, an Amen corner, and a harsh truth. Thank You

PREFACE

I pray this work finds you well, and if not, I pray it helps you get there!

FAMILY.

Lessons about life
Begin through the connections
Growth happens within

INFLUENCE.

Step out black girl, do it all on your own
You don't need a man for nothing, come sit on your throne
they are not gonna provide the things you want, so why waste your time.
You can raise those kids by yourself, who told you otherwise.
Your Momma did it, your Aunty did it, yall turned out fine, all off of what we provided, all men do is whine.
They cheat, they lie, they always got their hand out, complaining and asking me to pull a damn pot out.
Cook him a meal, cater to him, make him feel important.
Rub his back, open my legs, basically be a doormat.
I wish I would, as hard as I work, being the provider in yall life.
I'm strong and I'm independent, I can do without that strife.
I don't need a soul for a thing, even with dwindling health.

I smoke and drink the pain away; I can do this myself.
I'm just living my life, doing what's best for me.
This is the world for black women, not just me.
Wait till you get older, just wait and see.

MOMMA.

The separation from you created the first fear, I wailed in despair
Searching
For smells, for touch, pleading for you to be there
Wanting
Your position is that of unknowing, attempting to grant me my peace
Showing
The examples you were given, not always so sweet
Accepting
What we don't have, and all that we do
Knowing
You will forever have me, and I will have you

POPS.

My pen will bleed these words on paper
Because it is with pain that I write
Defining a father through a broken heart
Searching for a little light
I can't explain my pain, because I'm not yours
sidelined the love I have for you out of respect
for your real daughters
But you left me, you left me too
Our love was incomplete
It was pieced together, it was strained, I'd say it
was unique.
You weren't a responsible parent to me; you
were barely a friend.
In my eyes you didn't know how or what to be,
but you tried over and over again.
What manner of man is this?! The kind that's
flawed and real, the kind that won't make nice
but who's gonna live how he feels.
Was told one too many times that I didn't have a
father, so I'll make you my Pops
I'll remember the moments of how we paired
and know I loved you a lot.

I'll remember you in secret and all the moments we shared.
I'll cry tears for you alone because with others I wouldn't dare.
I will honor your memory always and the kinship that we built.
I saw a different side of you, and with those memories I'll sit.

MOTHER.

The clock spins round and I cater to you
No pain, frustration, or ailment is greater than
you
My body depletes and I give unto you
My dreams interrupted yet I fill them with you
My personal moments have limits, yet I share
them with you
My money is fleeting yet I spare it for you
It's never really enough but I find more for you
My coughs left unmanaged, but I find cures for
you
Most often without Thank Yous, and the
appreciation is scarce
I shed tears in the darkness, knowing honestly
that there's
not one single day I would think of rewinding
the time
to a minute or a second when you aren't mine

FEMININE.

Breathe. Take your time. Move with grace.
Know your position. Present a pleasant face.
Let your words be filled with assurance, but
don't be too loud.
Make heads turn when you walk in the room, try
not to be too proud.
Know the rules but play to win.
Let the Universe guide your steps.
Connect to all things from within.
Let your body be your sacred temple.
Blessed be the fruit.
Reserve your energy for the wars.
Let your battles be minute.
From your tongue bleeds the venom and also the
beauty of life.
You giveth and you taketh, such is your will and
your might.

LOVER.

Giving of myself
As I nurture from within
Through passion and Love

IX

A Friday night connection to YOU that led to a
Saturday devotion to conversation
On Sunday I saw the light that is YOU and the
reflection of things said and unsaid
Then the Monday blues and a longing for YOU
Tuesday to YOU I go to do the things that
soothe the ache of being away from YOU
Wednesday the feelings ring true, and I am
deeply attuned to YOU
Thursday, I relish in the side effects from the
love of my Muse who's YOU
Made Friday into the day when our bodies
connect, deepening our roots into each other at a
pace that only Mother Nature can
create........YOU
Sunday, I pulled away from your grasp only
enough to come up for air.
The space we share, now sacred, waiting for our
return.
Our love placed delicately there along with care
and ....YOU

SPELL.

Moving confidently
I see your face
Unknown powers
I move with grace
In your presence it starts
My core starts to burn
I can't find my heart
There begins the yearn
Spell
Your lips drip the poison that's taken my heart
Why can't I let go, I was yours from the start
One more time
Told you and myself that it stops here
You smile at me
My pleading falls on deaf ears
I can't do this with you, I want to run
To be honest, I can't leave til' you're done
Release me now
Let me out
I can't begin to think about my life without,
you lifting me up with your constant charm.
Overflowing on love, I'm beginning to drown.
You watch me intent as I accept my fate.
Not knowing the monster this spell creates.

FLOWHER.

The light peeks through
She opens for you
Morning dew drips from her lips inviting you in
The curves of her petals resting around your skin
You start to see her colors; she blooms open in
two
Passion unbridled as she consumes you
Your place in her garden is all you need
This flowher is your prize, come give into she

ENTER.

The sun rises
I'm realizing
that you're not here
Mesmerizing
thoughts of you seem to stay here
Only you can take it away
the longing desires
I open up you cum inside
Hold me when its time
let me go when it's not
Peace escapes my body, as soon as we stop
Won't be long now, the passion is so true
Addiction is the name for you
Enter my veins, but do it slow
Consume my body Baby, and don't let go
Rush to take me, slow to go
I fall when you leave, please don't go
Friends look at me funny, cuz I differ so much
I tell them you've taken me, it's a spell from your
touch
You think it's all lies, when I put those feels in
the air
I smile cuz you don't know, the obsession is
there

EXIT.

Loving you had a condition
I was not willing to pay
Suggesting was to differ
Separation causing pain
I wanted something deeper
On the surface we float
I knew we had to end
I was scared to rock the boat
I made an exit
Left you dreaming on the waves
I kept some love and affection
I drifted alone beside you to stay
I made an exit
Because I knew
The conditions of our love
Would cost me You
Confusion and pain
Fear everywhere
Wanting and needing you
Felt like a gift
Like my very air
Submerged in your body
Your beauty so sweet
I fought, I held tight
Needing your presence to sleep

I want you too much, incomplete without you
near
The fear of losing you, panic fills the air
Why does this feel scary?
Why can't I focus
Losing myself in this connection, I'm beginning
to choke its.......
Got a condition
That I'm not willing to pay
So, I climb out of our dream
And drift beside you to stay

UNIVERSE.

The Oneness calls me.
I succumb to life and death.
There is no pain here.

DEPTH.

Come to me when all else fails
I am the unseen strength
Lay within my depth
Unconsciously you feed me
The pain my most nurturing meal
Lay within my depth
The colors of emotion
Create a prism of pride within my flow
Lay within my depth
Let me speak through you
and lift you up
I emerge beneath the noise and with the soul
I am peace, I am the depth

UNCONDITIONAL.

From a place of pain my pen rings true.
Accepting everything I dare not change in you.
Laying judgement at my feet, lest my own flaws show up to defeat.
Eye to eye we face, seeing souls so displaced.
A fight neither one of us win, our hearts dangerously close to not trying again.
I want more than you are able to give, you want nothing more than I have given.
My needs show up and I constantly reflect.
Work on myself and not you, and the completion I will get.

HEAVENLY.

On bended knee I ask of thee
To give and show me grace
To forgive of me all my wrongs and let me in this place
My plate is full my cup is empty
I ask for you to fill it up
Remove the burdens left upon me
Please get me out this rut
My grandma prayed; my momma prayed
I'm just following suit
Our future lies in the hands of you
I know that you can do it
Even though their lives didn't change, and fortune never showed
We are blessed and highly favored but only God knows
Just pray and pray and pray and pray and please make sure you tithe
Be born again don't indulge in sin, keep it up and you'll survive
You'll fight to see another day on the battlefield of the Lord
Faith in you will get us what we need Heaven will be the reward

FOUR.

My Dearest Em, Meech, Summer, and Donte. I have insomnia and I'm left with my thoughts. As a mother I have not always felt successful, and I have been lost most of the time. One thing I know for certain though, I wanted all of you born in this realm happy and healthy. I did not care what went right or wrong, I knew that love would always guide me, and you would always feel it. I have downright sucked at being at Mom at sometimes, but the love and dedication is always there. The beauty I see in all of you keeps me in awe at all times. I will always choose you. Even when the relationships with your fathers crumbled in front of me, I kept my eyes on you. You are the best parts of me even when I couldn't see them in myself.

SWEETFACE.

You came at a time when darkness was
surrounding my very cause.
I held on to what little light I had and carried it
without pause.
I looked at myself 1000 times, outward and in.
You told me perfection was me and I would
never feel alone again.
I fought against our Love and didn't believe it to
be true.
You helped me trust, you held me there and
showed me all of you.
The love grew so deep most times I thought that
I would drown.
You stayed right there with me even until now.
Without you isn't a position that I ever want to
hold.
My Sweetface you are everything and this Love
will never grow old

www.ingramcontent.com/pod-product-compliance
Lightning Source LLC
Chambersburg PA
CBHW051718130826
49812CB00034B/1246
9789395784108